Trauma, Love, and Life

Nicholas Graham

Presentation by *BookLeaf Publishing*

Web: www.bookleafpub.com

E-mail: info@bookleafpub.com

ISBN: 9789357447881

First edition 2022

DEDICATION

This book is dedicated to 18 year old me. Someone who was thoughtful, engaged, and loving, despite having every right to be bitter, angry, and full of shame. This book was probably something you never thought possible, but we are going to get some of our work out there now.

ACKNOWLEDGEMENT

To Danielle Gibson, thank you for continuing to push me to channel my creativity into my work. This book would not have been possible had I not seen the way you exercise your creativity.

"Unused creativity is not benign. It metastasizes." - Brene Brown.

Ode to my Favorite Shirt

Laughter and joy poured out whenever you were
on me,
Unlike any rapture, I had previously known,
You took me fishing, on the river, on the boat,
you were there,
I took you golfing, every bogey, every stroke
you were there,
But after the move, we were separated and I was
lost,
High and low I searched for you, could it be that
you were searching for me too?
"Of course not," people said, you were "just a
shirt" they pleaded.
But now, 10 years later you do find me, you are
dirtier now though,
Holes cover your surface, not to mention you are
about three sizes too small,
It's like you need me more than I need you,
I tried to convince myself that you are worthy of
forgiveness, forgiveness for leaving me cold,
As if it wasn't your main responsibility to keep
me warm.

And the thing is, I do forgive you, but I just don't
see how you could ever fit on me again.
So instead of wearing you around, I'll hang you
up in my closet for nobody to see,
Nobody but me.

Generational Healing

It's been ten years since my father has lived with me,
Never taught me how to shave but do you see any cuts on me?
That man is lucky he lives in a separate town,
That man is lucky I never see him around,
'Cuz after all, I am a product of his seed,
And his anger and his hatred grow inside me,
But see, I'm just a little better at hiding,
Because I don't let alcohol describe me.
I promise you, my kids will never grow up without a father,
Down the aisle, I will walk my daughter,
I'll be there for my son and his soon to be wife,
While he's in his tux and she's dressed in white,
I'll smile at him, and he'll smile too,
All while the flower girl throws pedals down the pews.

Can't Beat Your Temper

I heard the anger spew from his face
As his empty whiskey bottle smashed to the
hardwood below.
Thump, thump, thump...
I heard his livid legs slosh closer to my room.
Thump, thump, thump...
I retreat into the sanctuary of my sheets.
Thump, thump, thump...
I heard that helped keep monsters away.
Thump, thump, thump...
I heard the strength of my guardian doorknob
crack under his pressure.
Thump, thump, thump...

Burden

5

Her gaze welcomes me in,
Like an empty room begging to be furnished,
But I've come with no money,
And I've come with my burdens,
And now there's a glass wall in between us.

Insecurities

Why do my dreams invite my insecurities to
play?
I know I am better than the doubts wittily
whispered through my peaks,
But even a mountain can only withstand so
much pressure.

Wonder

The warmth of her heart melts away the arctic
dessert I've built around my soul.
In fairness to myself, I have been working on
climate change,
But it is so refreshing to meet someone that
makes that feel easy.
Her eyes wander deeply into my existence,
creating the existence of sheer wonder,
It's a special phenomenon when a connection
with someone can create certain wonder, a
comfortable wonder.
I wonder what it is about her laugh that makes
the butterflies in my stomach smile,
I wonder what it is about her voice that makes
me believe every word she says,
I wonder what it is about her eyes that hold me
accountable to live my truth,
I wonder what our living room would look like
in thirty years,
I wonder what it would sound like.
I wonder what it is that I did to deserve her in
my life.

Ants

It's unfortunate that you've run across me,
I have a reputation for crushing things like you,
I feel heartless for doing it,
But that is a cruel reminder that there is no easy
way to feel.

No Strings

No strings attached, well, no feelings at all,
Man, what would that even feel like?
That's not me, I'm the bartender that pours you
your drink for free,
Then watches as you spill your words on the
table,
And then cleans up the mess.
I'll walk you to your car,
Dropping pieces of my soul as you invite
someone else into the passenger seat.
It's okay, you go on and have fun, I got some
stuff to clean up here.

Forgetting

The hardest part about forgetting is the longing
to remember,
How can I forget the scars left on my brain?

The hardest part about forgetting is the
self-torture,
The shredding pain that comes with the
abandonment of once cherished memories,

The hardest part about forgetting is realizing that
it isn't losing the memories that hurt,
It is the thought of losing the validation of your
self-worth received from those memories.

Once you realize that, you'll quickly find that
you no longer need to forget,
You need to figure out why your past self holds
more value than present you.

Void

I told them about the void that appeared when
you didn't,
Guess what?
It didn't help.

The Pharaoh's Servant

I was once told about a Pharaoh's servant whose only job was to be covered in honey.
The honey attracted the locust and that meant the Pharaoh didn't get inconvenienced by the insect's presence.
I remember thinking that there was a point in my life where I would have volunteered for that job to benefit the people I loved.
I'm not totally convinced that I would turn the job down today if asked.
I do know that the people-pleasing persona of my past no longer aligns with my best of standards.
My best of standards makes me the Pharaoh of my life.
Not necessarily forcing inconvenience on others,
Just not accepting inconvenience of self to benefit others.

Queens and Onstott

You stole my jacket and my heart and threw
them both down the gutter on the corner of
Queens and Onstott
You sped off down the wrong road,
But my beat-up four-cylinder didn't have the
power to
Intercept the conflicting emotions that
intoxicated your mind.
I guess that explains the alcohol.
I fought for you... No, I fight for you,
But my fists have no effect on the opponent
When the opponent is just a silhouette of the
person you've become,
They just bounce off or shatter, like a rock
against glass.
My words echo out but everyone around is deaf
because they never took the time out of their life
for you as I did,
The words that come out of my mouth are mute
to my own ears because my ears can't see you
the way my eyes do, and my eyes don't see you
as much as I'd like them to.

Just Dance

I wish I was able to be the first person on the
dance floor.
I'm not sure what scares me more,
The thought of being the subject of everyone's
jokes,
Or the thought of the pure joy that dancing
without care would bring.
The unhinged feeling of freedom.

Side Note

Side note, I want to slow dance with you,
I'm not sure why, but I feel my heart longing for
it.
I want your arms around my shoulders,
I want my hands on your waist,
I want a song playing that makes our mouth
smile.
Side note, you are amazing.

A Stale Glass of Water

I only reach for you because I know you are all I
have,
Sitting on my nightstand, just as I left you,
Just as I planned the night before,
Day-old water might as well be the best thing on
earth after drinking,
Still, why do I only find you refreshing after a
night of bad decisions?

Delimma

I am stuck between a rock and a hard place.
The rock is comfort and the hard place is joy,
I've had my shell broken so many times,
it's hard to walk out into the open.
My brain says move forward,
My gut knows what will happen when I do,
My heart says move forward,
My bones ache because they know they can't
take any more abuse.
How do you manage caution with progress?

Heartland

I whistled with the Western Wind while walking
down my newly beaten path,
I am heading south.
I've lived up North for so long, you could say
I've been stuck in my head.
I'm moving to the heartland.
A place where people who wear their hearts on
their sleeves are talked about as heroes.

Golden Coast - Haiku

Rolling Hills of Gold
Met with demanding green leaves
Perfect Harmony

Goosebumps

Goosebumps were meant to ward off predators,
So why do I get them when I look at you?
Am I that afraid of how badly you could hurt
me?